ISBN 978-0-9557183-0-04

ASR Ink would like to extend their thanks to Shabnam, Shahnaz, Sabreen, Ayesha, Maeesha, Hassan, Lamisa, Natasha, Adnan and all the adults that took on the 99 Club© Challenge in August 2007 and successfully learnt the 99 beautiful names of Allah (SWT). It was because of your efforts that we were inspired to write this book. May Allah (SWT) shower his blessings upon you.

A Gift for:

Message:

From:

Date:

The 99 Names of Allah Workbook

Learn the 99 Names of Allah and gain His pleasure

"Allah is He, beside Whom there is no other god;
Who knows both what is hidden and what can be witnessed;
He is the Most Compassionate and Merciful.
Allah is He, other than Whom there is no other god;
The King, the Holy, the Source of Peace,
The Guardian of Faith, the Preserver of Security,
The Mighty, the Compeller, the Majestic.
Glorified is Allah, beyond any associations.
He is Allah, the Creator, the Evolver, the Bestower of Form.
To Him belong the Most Beautiful Names:
Whatever exists in heaven and earth declares His Praise and Glory.
And He is All Mighty in Power, the All Wise".

Quran: Surah 59, verses 22-24

Dedicated to the memory of our dear father, Habib Ullah Bakht and beloved brother, Ahmed Iqbal

peace be upon them

Introduction

At the start of the summer holidays in 2007, we decided to set a challenge for our children to learn the 99 names of Allah. We didn't want them to spend weeks of monotony and return to school, numb from the lack of use of their brain. They would have something constructive to show for the holidays and instead of returning to school in September saying how bored they had been; this year was going to be different!

We started by setting the children a goal to aim for; this was a surprise that would only be revealed at the end of successfully learning the 99 names. We then set a learning programme that was realistic, manageable and achievable, intended to sustain learning without becoming tedious. What ensued was a surprise to us all. The children rose to the challenge without a fuss - in fact they were immensely excited and before we knew it, 7 other children had also taken on the challenge along with 7 adults, all across Scotland and England! Our ages ranged from 6 to 45 years.

Everyone worked together, to support each other to learn and before we knew it, we were seeking innovative ways of teaching our group. We developed worksheets and exercises, set targets, practised together, encouraged and motivated each other with the rewards that lay ahead, namely the blessings of Allah and a big surprise. At regular intervals we would give the children small incentives to keep them motivated as well as giving them breaks if they were tired or became distracted. Our total learning time per day was approximately 30 minutes - not much when you consider that at the end of the learning period, there were real measurable results.

As the weeks progressed, we discovered that our children were motivated and enthusiastic about learning, keen for the rewards, and they were developing a sense of satisfaction each time they reached a milestone. We realised this occurred because the practise was manageable and on a daily basis with regular repetition. We felt compelled to share this with others with the aim of promoting a love of acquiring Islamic knowledge, accessible to all through simple learning techniques and, most importantly, as a means of developing an international community of learners who all aspire to the same goal. Lifelong learning is important in Islam, for Allah (SWT) says, "travel to the ends of the earth in search of knowledge".

We aim now to encourage others, both adults and children, to learn by sharing tried and tested methods and gain Allah's (SWT) pleasure. We are dedicated to encouraging others to benefit from our insight as well as from any funds we raise through the sale of this workbook. That is why we have developed the 99 Club© Trust Fund, which originated to help those less fortunate than ourselves both in the UK and abroad. We feel sure that you will find this resource refreshingly different.

We hope you find this toolkit an uncomplicated, constructive resource and ultimately, gain reward from our Creator for your efforts. Our mistakes are our own (may Allah (SWT) forgive us) and our success is due to the blessings of the Almighty. May He grant us all peace and success in this life and in the Hereafter.

Ameen.

Contents

How to use the Workbook

Preparation for everyone who is participating in the challenge is important, whether that is an individual or groups. Everyone needs to understand the aims, objectives and expectations of what they are undertaking. It should not be seen as a punishment and therefore should be presented in a non-threatening manner. For us, we presented it as a non-competitive challenge with a reward at the end for the whole group, adults and children alike.

For Groups

The group leader should learn alongside the group members. This motivates the learners and encourages them to continue as well as giving the leader an insight into the learning experience of the individuals. **The following process needs to be explained to the group.**

- The reason for taking on the challenge
- The goals to be achieved at each stage
- The benefits of taking on the challenge
- The incentives that will be provided along the way e.g. a small treat every time 30 names have been memorized.
- The reward at the end of the process. **Try to keep this a mystery to maintain interest.**

For Individuals

Individuals need to be motivated to learn. Children who are learning on an individual basis should be supervised by an adult to ensure that goals and targets are being timely met and to offer support and guidance throughout the process. Most parents find that they begin to learn with their children.

Use the cards provided regularly. Take them with you wherever you go and get them out to practise whenever you have a spare minute. We've used them when commuting and standing in queues to name but a few!

For Parents

It is important that parents are patient and supportive throughout the learning process to avoid the child experiencing a negative learning experience. The Challenge should be presented in a non-threatening manner and positive encouragement should be offered throughout. Consider learning alongside your child; it will make the experience less daunting for your child and have other positive relationship benefits. Ensure that a goal is set and that incentives are offered at regular intervals e.g. a special outing or inexpensive gift each time 33 names have been learnt. Consider having a special celebration at the end of the Challenge to share your child's success with others.

Participants need to be aware of the process and what is involved. The following is important to note.

- One workbook per learner is necessary.
- The target to complete the challenge should be set at the outset, although it is possible to work at an individual pace if desired.
- Users should work through each section methodically.

- The progress chart should be used to monitor progress.
- At all times, if users find they have not learnt the expected number of names, they should go back and revise the relevant names.
- For group and individual learners, it is recommended to have incentives at regular periods, perhaps after successful completion of each section, to maintain the momentum.
- Once all the names have been successfully learnt, the certificates, provided in the book, should be presented to the learner/s. A 99 Club© Ceremony would be a final recognition of the effort and success of the learners.

When Problems Occur

As this is real life, issues will arise whilst you are learning, such as work may be missed for a few days or a week. This is okay; just add on the missed names to the list that needs to be learnt. If you are going on holiday, keep up with the work. 3 names a day or 1 a day is not such a hardship when you think of the gains and if done positively, makes it an enjoyable experience. Why should working for the sake of Allah be a chore? All play and no work makes a dull child! Or adult.

Lamisa - Case Study

8 year old Lamisa learnt 3 names a day alongside her 11 year old sister and mother. She spent 20 minutes a day in the morning learning 3 names a day, using the exercises, then 15 minutes re-capping names already learnt. Her mother would then test both children verbally for 10 minutes and they in turn would sometimes test their mother when she was driving, using the postcard-sized cards as a resource. Each day's new names would be added to the cards. When they learnt 30 names they received a small gift and again at the 60-name stage. Lamisa also practiced with her cousins. She received encouragement from her extended family via the telephone and letters in the post and this helped her to persevere. Alhamdulillah, at the end of the 6-week period, she had learnt the 99 Names of Allah and she still practices them in order to maintain her knowledge.

How and Why?

We believe this method works because the goals are short term, achievable and as a result concentration levels can be sustained better. Children are easily motivated because they know there is a reward at the end of the process. It is an excellent team building exercise and improves both family and group bonds if adults/children/groups take up the challenge together. This workbook is highly recommended to teach children as it gives them a positive learning experience and thus will encourage them to continue with further Islamic learning and provides them with a great belief in their own abilities.

Ready to Begin?

1. Start by removing the certificate and keep it in a safe place, ready for when you present it to your child or yourself, if the book is for you.
2. Carefully cut out the cards as directed.
3. Begin the written exercises on page 21.
4. You've done it.

You have now begun the process of learning Allah's 99 Names, Insha-Allah.

Study Programme

The amount of time required to succeed in learning the 99 names will depend on the chosen programme of study and the effort put into adhering to this programme. The table below gives you an **approximate** example of the various options. These learning times are based on average ability and will require the individual to be diligent and meticulous in their approach to learning if success is to be achieved. The key is to select a learning programme that suits the individual's needs and is realistic and achievable i.e. do not attempt to learn all 99 names in 3 weeks if you know you do not have the recommended time to devote each day to learning! However, learners can choose not to follow a fixed programme of learning and work at their own pace. You know what you are capable of, but nothing beats a little competitive spirit! Challenge yourself.

Number of weeks	Approx number of names to learn	Approx amount of time per day	Total learning time per day
6 Weeks	2 per day	20 minutes + 10 to recap	30 Minutes
5 Weeks	3 per day	30 minutes + 15 to recap	45 Minutes
4 Weeks	4 per day	40 minutes + 20 to recap	60 Minutes
3 Weeks	5 per day	50 minutes + 30 to recap	1 Hr 20 Minutes

Study will consist of the following learning methods:

- **Repetition** – practising the names using written worksheets
- **Memorisation** – oral recitation of the 99 names
- **Worksheets** – written exercises to support learning
- **Puzzles** - to consolidate learning
- **Mind Map** – To assess progress at the end of each section
- **Cards** - to be carried around and used at convenient times

At all times, the learner must be focused on achieving results. For children, it is important that an adult supervises their progress and offers support, positive encouragement and praise. Parents/adults will know their children/group best. Choose an appropriate place, time and pace. Consolidation of the names learnt is paramount to success and practise, practise, practise is the key. Nowhere is it more appropriate to say that practise makes perfect!

For the purposes of learning, the names are listed at all times with a corresponding number. It is strongly recommended that the numbers of each name be memorised alongside the meaning. This is because the brain learns quicker by association and is able to quantify the 99 names and store them. Without the numbers, memorisation becomes haphazard. You will also be able to recall each name at random if you do this.

The 99 Names of Allah and Meaning

There are differing versions of the 99 names of Allah and some that suggest Allah's names are not in fact limited to 99. Some accounts suggest that there were inconsistencies amongst the various schools of thought. For the purposes of this workbook we have therefore adopted the list of 99 names most commonly found on Islamic publications. It should also be noted that it is not possible to accurately transliterate the names from Arabic into English due to the differences in language. The nearest transliteration has therefore been used.

^= letter ain of Arabic '= letter hamza of Arabic

Number	Name	Meaning
1	**Ar- Rahman** الرحمن	**The Compassionate**, The Beneficent, The One who has plenty of mercy for the believers and the blasphemers in this world and especially for the believers in the hereafter.
2	**Ar-Raheem** الرحيم	**The Merciful**, The One who has plenty of mercy for the believers.
3	**Al-Malik** الملك	**The King**, The Sovereign Lord, The One with the complete Dominion, the One Whose Dominion is clear from imperfection.
4	**Al-Qudoos** القـدوس	**The Holy**, The One who is pure from any imperfection and clear from children and adversaries.
5	**As-Salaam** السـلام	**The Source of Peace**, The One who is free from every imperfection.
6	**Al-Mu'min** المـؤمن	**Guardian of Faith**, The One who witnessed for Himself that no one is God but Him. And He witnessed for His believers that they are truthful in their belief that no one is God but Him.
7	**Al-Muhaimin** المهيمن	**The Protector**, The One who witnesses the speech and deeds of His creatures
8	**Al-^Azeez** العـزيز	**The Mighty**, The Strong, The Defeater who is not defeated.
9	**Al-Jabbar** الجبـار	**The Compeller**, The One in whose dominion nothing happens except that which He wills.
10	**Al-Mutakabbir** المتكـبر	**The Majestic**, The One who is above the attributes of His creatures and who does not resemble them.

11	**Al-Khaaliq** الخالق	**The Creator**, The One who brings everything from non-existence to existence.
12	**Al-Bari'** البارئ	**The Evolver**, The Maker, The Creator who has the power to turn the entities.
13	**Al-Musawwir** المصور	**The Fashioner**, The One who forms His creatures in different pictures.
14	**Al-Ghaffaar** الغفار	**The Great Forgiver**, The Forgiver, The One who forgives the sins of His slaves time and time again.
15	**Al-Qahaar** القهار	**The Subduer**, The Dominant, The One who has the perfect power and for whom nothing is impossible.
16	**Al-Wahaab** الوهاب	**The Bestower**, The One who is Generous in giving plenty without any return. He is everything that benefits whether halal or haram.
17	**Ar-Razzaaq** الرزاق	**The Sustainer**, The Provider.
18	**Al-Fattaah** الفتاح	**The Opener**, The Reliever, The Judge, The One who opens for His slaves the closed worldly and religious matters.
19	**Al-^Aleem** العليم	**The All-knowing**, The Knowledgeable; The One from whose knowledge nothing is absent.
20	**Al-Qaabid** القابض	**The Constricter**, The Retainer, The Withholder, The One who constricts the sustenance by His wisdom and expands and widens it with His generosity and mercy.
21	**Al-Baasit** الباسط	**The Expander**, The Englarger, The One who constricts the sustenance by His wisdom and expands and widens it with His generosity and mercy.
22	**Al-Khaafid** الخافض	**The Abaser**, The One who lowers whoever He wills by His destruction and raises whoever He wills by His endowment.
23	**Ar-Raafi^** الرافع	The Exhalter. The Elevator. The One who lowers whoever He wills by His destruction and raises whoever He wills by His endowment.
24	**Al-Mu^iz** المعز	**The Honorer**, He gives esteem to whoever He wills, hence there is no one to degrade Him; And He degrades whoever He wills, hence there is no one to give Him esteem.

25	**Al-Muthil** المذل	**The Dishonorer**, The Humiliator, He gives esteem to whoever He wills, hence there is no one to degrade Him; and He degrades whoever He willed, hence there is no one to give Him esteem.
26	**As-Samee^** السميع	**The All-Hearing**, The Hearer, The One who Hears all things that are heard by His Eternal Hearing without an ear, instrument or organ.
27	**Al-Baseer** البصير	**The All-Seeing**, The One who Sees all things that are seen by His Eternal Sight without a pupil or any other instrument.
28	**Al-Hakam** الحكم	**The Judge**, He is the Ruler and His judgment is His word.
29	**Al-^Adl** العدل	**The Just**, The One who is entitled to do what He does.
30	**Al-Lateef** اللطيف	**The Subtle One**, The Gracious, The One who is kind to His slaves and endows them with blessings.
31	**Al-Khabeer** الخبير	**The Aware**, The One who knows the truth of things.
32	**Al-Haleem** الحليم	**The Forbearing**, The Clement, The One who delays the punishment for those who deserve it and who may then forgive them
33	**Al-^Azeem** العظيم	**The Great One**, The Mighty, The One deserving the attributes of Exaltation, Glory, Praise, and Purity from all imperfection
34	**Al-Ghafoor** الغفور	**The All-Forgiving**, The Forgiving, The One who forgives a lot.
35	**Ash-Shakoor** الشكور	**The Grateful**, The Appreciative, The One who gives a lot of reward for a little obedience.
36	**Al-^Aliyy** العلي	**The Most High**, The Sublime, The One who is clear from the attributes of the creatures.
37	**Al-Kabeer** الكبير	**The Most Great**, The Great, The One who is greater than everything in status.
38	**Al-Hafeez** الحفيظ	**The Preserver**, The Protector, The One who protects whatever and whoever it is his will to protect.

39	**Al-Muqeet** المقيـــت	**The Maintainer**, The Guardian, The Feeder, The Sustainer, The One who has the Power.
40	**Al-Haseeb** الحســـيب	**The Reckoner**, The One who gives the satisfaction.
41	**Aj-Jaleel** الجليـــل	**The Sublime One**, The Beneficent, The One who is attributed with greatness of power and glory of status.
42	**Al-Kareem** الكـــريم	**The Generous One**, The Bountiful, The Gracious, The One who is attributed with greatness of power and glory of status.
43	**Ar-Raqeeb** الرقيـــب	**The Watcher**, The Watchful, The One from whom nothing is absent.
44	**Al-Mujeeb** المجيـــب	**The Responsive**, The Hearkener, The One who answers the one in need if he asks Him and rescues the yearner if he calls upon Him.
45	**Al-Wasi^** الواســـع	**The Vast**, The All-Embracing, The Knowledgeable.
46	**Al-Hakeem** الحكيـــم	**The Wise**, The Judge of Judges, The One who is correct in His doings.
47	**Al-Wadood** الـودود	**The Loving**, The One who loves His believing slaves and His believing slaves love Him. His love to His slaves is His will to be merciful to them and praise them.
48	**Al-Majeed** المجيـــد	**The Most Glorious One**, The Glorious, The One who is with perfect power, high status, compassion, generosity and kindness.
49	**Al-Ba^ith** الباعـــث	**The Resurrector**, The Raiser (from death), The One who resurrects His slaves after death for reward and/or punishment.
50	**Ash-Shaheed** الشـــهيد	**The Witness**, The One from whom nothing is absent.
51	**Al-Haqq** الحـق	**The Truth**, The True, The One who truly exists.
52	**Al-Wakeel** الوكيـــل	**The Trustee**, The One who gives satisfaction and is relied upon.

53	**Al-Qawiyy** القـــوى	**The Most Strong**, The Strong, The One with the complete power.
54	**Al-Mateen** المتيـــــن	**The Firm One**, The One with extreme power which is uninterrupted. He does not tire.
55	**Al-Waliyy** الولـــى	**The Protecting Friend**, The Supporter.
56	**Al-Hameed** الحميـــد	**The Praiseworthy**, The praised One who deserves to be praised.
57	**Al-Muhsee** المحصـــى	**The Counter**, The Reckoner, The One to whom the count of things is known.
58	**Al-Mubdi'** المبـــدئ	**The Originator**, The One who started the human being. That is, He created him.
59	**Al-Mu^eed** المعيـــد	**The Reproducer**, The One who brings back the creatures after death.
60	**Al-Muhyi** المحـــيى	**The Restorer**, The Giver of Life, The One who took out a living human from semen that does not have a soul. He gives life by giving the souls back to the worn out bodies on the resurrection day and He makes the hearts alive by the light of knowledge.
61	**Al-Mumeet** المميـــت	**The Creator of Death**, The Destroyer, The One who renders the living dead.
62	**Al-Hayy** الحـــى	**The Alive**, The One attributed with a life that is unlike our life and is not that of a combination of soul, flesh or blood.
63	**Al-Qayyoom** القيـــوم	**The Self-Subsisting**, The One who remains and does not end.
64	**Al-Wajid** الواجـد	**The Perceiver**, The Finder, The Rich who is never poor. Al-Wajid is Richness.
65	**Al-Majid** الماجـد	**The Illustrious**, The Magnificent.
66	**Al-Wahid** الواحـد	**The Unique**, The One, The One without a partner.

67	**Al-Ahad** الاحد	**The One,** The All Inclusive, The Indivisible.
68	**As-Samad** الصمد	**The Eternal**, The Independent, The Master who is relied upon in matters and reverted to in one's needs.
69	**Al-Qaadir** القادر	**The Able**, The Capable, The One attributed with Power.
70	**Al-Muqtadir** المقتدر	**The Powerful**, The Dominant, The One with the perfect power from whom nothing is withheld.
71	**Al-Muqaddim** المقدم	**The Expediter**, The Promoter, The One who puts things in their rightful places. He brings forward what He wills and delays what He wills.
72	**Al-Mu'akh-khir** المؤخر	The **Delayer.** The One who puts things in their rightful places. He brings forward what He wills and delays what He wills.
73	**Al-'Awwal** الأول	**The First**, The One whose Existence is without a beginning.
74	**Al-'Akhir** الأخر	**The Last**, The One whose Existence is without an end.
75	**Az-Zaahir** الظاهر	**The Manifest**. Nothing is above Him and nothing is underneath Him, hence He exists without a place. His existence is obvious by proofs.
76	**Al-Baatin** الباطن	**The Hidden**, Nothing is above Him and nothing is underneath Him, hence He exists without a place. His existence is obvious by proofs.
77	**Al-Walee** الوالي	**The Governor**, The One who owns things and manages them.
78	**Al-Muta^ali** المتعالي	**The Most Exalted**, The High, Exhalted, the One who is clear from the attributes of creation.
79	**Al-Barr** البر	**The Source of All Goodness**, The Righteous, The One who is kind to His creatures, who covered them with His sustenance and favoured whoever He willed among them by His support, protection, and special mercy.
80	**At-Tawwaab** التواب	**The Acceptor of Repentance**, The Relenting, The One who grants repentance to whoever He wills among His creatures and accepts his repentance.

81	**Al-Muntaqim** المنتقم	**The Avenger**, The One who victoriously prevails over His enemies and punishes them for their sins. It may mean the One who destroys them.
82	**Al-^Afuww** العفو	**The Pardoner**, The Forgiver, The One with vast forgiveness.
83	**Ar-Ra'uf** الرؤوف	**The Compassionate**, The One with extreme mercy. The mercy of Allah is His will to bless whoever He wills among His creatures.
84	**Malik Al-Mulk** مالك الملك	**The Eternal Owner of Sovereignty**, The One who controls the Dominion and gives dominion to whoever He willed.
85	**Thul-Jalali wal-Ikram** ذو الجلال و الإكرام	**The Lord of Majesty and Bounty**, The One who deserves to be Exalted and not denied.
86	**Al-Muqsit** المقسط	**The Equitable**, The One who is just in His judgment.
87	**Aj-Jaami^** الجامع	**The Gatherer**, The One who gathers the creatures on a day of which there is no doubt, that is, the Day of Judgment
88	**Al-Ghaniyy** الغني	**The Self-Sufficient**, The One who does not need the creation.
89	**Al-Mughni** المغني	**The Enricher**, The One who satisfies the necessities of the creatures.
90	**Al-Maani^** المانع	**The Preventer**, The Withholder.
91	**Ad-Daarr** الضار	**The Distresser**, The One who makes harm reach whoever He wills and benefits whoever He wills.
92	**An-Nafi^** النافع	**The Benefactor**, The One who makes harm reach whoever He wills and benefits whoever He wills.
93	**An-Noor** النور	**The Light**, The One who guides.
94	**Al-Haadi** الهادي	**The Guide**, The One with whose Guidance His believers are guided to what is beneficial for them and protected from what is harmful to them.

95	**Al-Badi^** البـــــديع	**The Incomparable**, The One who created the creation and formed it without any preceding example.
96	**Al-Baaqi** البـــــاقي	**The Everlasting**, The One for whom the state of non-existence is impossible .
97	**Al-Waarith** الوارث	**The Supreme Inheritor**, The Heir, The One whose Existence remains.
98	**Ar-Rasheed** الرشــــــيد	**The Guide to the Right Path**, The One who guides.
99	**As-Saboor** الصــــــبور	**The Patient**, The One who does not quickly punish the sinners.

Advice On Encouraging Learning

This workbook is aimed at children and adults alike. We do however recommend that children are supervised by an adult during the learning process. As children are easily distracted, we suggest the following to achieve success:

- Have a dedicated time each day to learn the target numbers of names. This will depend on the choice of learning programme and your daily commitments. However, work should be done preferably each day in order to consolidate learning.
- Avoid television, radio and other distractions.
- Children should be supervised when learning.
- Adults could consider learning alongside children as this will inspire and motivate them to learn. Parents can rightfully feel proud of their children when they themselves have gone through the same process.
- It helps if more than one child is learning at the same time so encourage siblings, friends or relatives to join in, no matter what their age. Knowledge has no limits or age.
- Make sure children are not hungry or tired e.g. before bedtime is inappropriate.
- Children should be given a reward at the end of each learning session. A kiss and genuine appreciation of their *efforts* will suffice.
- Children should be encouraged with praise and positive feedback.
- Avoid negative comments if children are not progressing as expected. Always appreciate the efforts they are making.
- Praise, praise, praise is the key.
- Motivate them to learn by having a special celebration once all the names have been learnt. Consider having a 99 Names celebration where others can be invited, a recital could be given, certificates and medals awarded. Children will feel immensely proud that their efforts have been recognised and rewarded not only at home but in the wider community. Shout it out!
- Consider using other learning materials available from the 99 Club© to support their learning such as additional worksheets and flash cards.

Exercises

Depending on whether you are working at your own pace or following a fixed programme of study, worksheets will need to be completed on a regular basis and oral memorisation will need to be practised, preferably on a daily basis. This could be as little as five minutes a day to 15 minutes per day depending on the number of names you are leaning. The workbook is divided into 3 main learning sections, each section focusing on learning 33 names. Each section consists of practise worksheets to encourage memorisation, name and number recognition worksheets, puzzles and word searches to build on knowledge, and mind maps to consolidate learning at the end of each section.

Study Routine

First stage of learning – Written lists & oral memorisation

1. Write out each name ten times and recite the names as you write. The memorisation lists will help you.
2. Write the names you are learning onto the cards each day as you go along. Don't write them out all in one day! Then read out the names at least ten times. Practise both forwards and in reverse order.
3. Write out all the names that you know in order, with number, name and meaning.- without help. Repeat until you can do this without any mistakes.
4. Update your progress chart.
5. Use the cards in your daily life to help with memorisation.

Second stage of learning – Number, Name and Meaning Recognition Worksheets

6. Complete the written worksheets. This will encourage name, meaning and number recognition.
7. Check and mark all correct answers against the list of 99 Names.
8. For any incorrect ones, write out the number, name and meaning 5 times each again.
9. Update your progress chart.

Third stage of learning- Test your knowledge

10. Once you have learnt 33 names in each section, you can test your knowledge by attempting the word search and puzzle.
11. Consolidate learning at the end of each section by completing the Mind Maps.
12. Regularly recite the names you have learnt and time yourself.
13. Keep a record of the times taken on the Memorisation Record.
14. Congratulate yourself/your child/your group and then take a break.

Fourth stage of learning – Final test

15. Complete the final test, set yourself a maximum time limit if you wish.
16. Mark your answers.
17. Insha'Allah, having followed this programme of learning, you will have achieved your goal.
18. Plan your 99 Club© celebration and share your newly acquired knowledge with others.

Progress Chart

Use the chart below to record your progress.

Section: 2, 3 or 4	Target names per day	Memorisation Worksheets completed	Oral memorisation completed	Puzzles completed	Word search completed	Mind Map Completed	Re-cap completed	Areas to work on

Memorisation List, Names 1 to 11

Start by practising the names of Allah in the following way.

1. Write each number, name and meaning 10 times and in order on a separate piece of paper.
2. Verbally recite each number, name and meaning out loud.
3. When you are confident you have memorised them, update the Progress Chart.

Number	Name	Meaning
1	Ar-Rahman	The Compassionate, the Beneficent
2	Ar-Raheem	The Merciful
3	Al-Malik	The King
4	Al-Qudoos	The Holy

Written exercise completed ☐ Oral Memorisation completed ☐ Progress chart completed ☐

Number	Name	Meaning
5	As-Salaam	The Source of Peace
6	Al-Mu'min	The Guardian of Faith
7	Al-Muhaimin	The Protector
8	Al-^Azeez	The Mighty

Written exercise completed ☐ Oral Memorisation completed ☐ Progress chart completed ☐

Number	Name	Meaning
9	Al-jabbar	The Compeller
10	Al-Mutakabbir	The Majestic
11	Al-Khaaliq	The Creator

Written exercise completed ☐ Oral Memorisation completed ☐ Progress chart completed ☐

Learning tip –

"Your brain is capable of multi-tasking! So walking or driving to the shops and practising the names of Allah in your head can easily be done." ***Mutasim, dad to 2***

"I think learning with someone else helped me to do my Names of Allah. I always worked with my dad." ***Natasha, 7***

Memorisation List, Names 12 to 22

Start by practising the names of Allah in the following way.

1. Write each number, name and meaning 10 times and in order on a separate piece of paper.
2. Verbally recite each number, name and meaning out loud.
3. When you are confident you have memorised them, update the Progress Chart.

Number	Name	Meaning
12	Al-Bari	The Evolver
13	Al-Musawwir	The Fashioner
14	Al-Ghaffar	The Great Forgiver
15	Al-Qahhaar	The Subduer

Written exercise completed ☐ Oral Memorisation completed ☐ Progress chart completed ☐

Number	Name	Meaning
16	Al-Wahhab	The Bestower
17	Al-Razzaaq	The Sustainer
18	Al-Fattaah	The Opener
19	Al-^Aleem	The All-Knowing

Written exercise completed ☐ Oral Memorisation completed ☐ Progress chart completed ☐

Number	Name	Meaning
20	Al-Qaabid	The Constrictor
21	Al-Baasit	The Expander
22	Al-Khaafid	The Abaser

Written exercise completed ☐ Oral Memorisation completed ☐ Progress chart completed ☐

Learning tip –

"I learnt best by getting together with my cousins every few days. We'd sit in my Grandma's conservatory, practise and then test each other verbally on numbers, names and meanings. It was great fun." ***Ayesha, 11***

Memorisation List, Names 23 to 33

Start by practising the names of Allah in the following way.

1. Write each number, name and meaning 10 times and in order on a separate piece of paper.
2. Verbally recite each number, name and meaning out loud.
3. When you are confident you have memorised them, update the Progress Chart.

Number	Name	Meaning
23	Ar-Raafi^	The Exalter
24	Al-Mu^iz	The Honorer
25	Al-Muthil	The Dishonorer
26	As-Samee^	The All-Hearing

Written exercise completed ☐ Oral Memorisation completed ☐ Progress chart completed ☐

Number	Name	Meaning
27	Al-Baseer	The All-Seeing
28	Al-Hakam	The Judge
29	Al-^Adl	The Just
30	Al-Lateef	The Subtle One

Written exercise completed ☐ Oral Memorisation completed ☐ Progress chart completed ☐

Number	Name	Meaning
31	Al-Khabeer	The Aware
32	Al-Haleem	The Forbearing
33	Al-^Azeem	The Most Great

Written exercise completed ☐ Oral Memorisation completed ☐ Progress chart completed ☐

Learning tip –

"When doing mundane tasks such as cutting vegetables or tidying up, recite the numbers, names and meanings in reverse order. It makes the time go quicker and really makes you think!"
Mahmuda, mum to 2

Name Recognition, Names 1 to 11

Complete the meanings of the names and check your answers against the list of names on pages 9. Note your correct and incorrect answers in the box.

1. Ar- Rahmaan	7. Al-Muhaimin	4. Al-Qudoos
5. As-Salaam	3. Al-Malik	6. Al-Mu'min
9. Al-Jabbar	8. Al-^Azeez	9. Al-Khaliq
10. Al-Mutakabbir	2. Ar-Raheem	**Correct** ☐ **Incorrect** ☐

Write the missing number and Arabic name for each meaning

. The Source of Peace	. The Majestic	. The Merciful
. The Protector	. The Holy	. The Compassionate the Beneficent
. The Mighty	. The King	. The Guardian of Faith
. The Creator	. The Compeller	**Correct** ☐ **Incorrect** ☐

Cover the above 2 exercises and then write the correct names with meaning next to each number in the box below.

5.	3.	8.
9.	4.	1.
6.	7.	2.
11.	10.	**Correct** ☐ **Incorrect** ☐

Name Recognition, Names 12 to 22

Complete the meanings of the names and check your answers against the list of names on pages 10. Note your correct and incorrect answers in the box.

20. Al-Qaabid	15. Al-Qahhaar	12. Al-Bari
21. Al-Baasit	13. Al-Musawwir	17. Ar-Razzaaq
14. Al-Ghaffaar	16. Al-wahaab	19. Al- Aleem
22. Al-Khaafid	18. Al-Fattaah	**Correct** ☐ **Incorrect** ☐

Write the missing number and Arabic name for each meaning

.The Bestower	.The Constrictor	.The Great Forgiver
.The Fashioner	.The Sustainer	.The Evolver
.The Subduer	.The Creator	.The Majestic
.The All Knowing	.The Abaser	**Correct** ☐ **Incorrect** ☐

Cover the above 2 exercises and then write the correct names with meaning next to each number in the box below.

19.	12.	21.
16.	22.	14.
18.	20.	15.
13.	17.	**Correct** ☐ **Incorrect** ☐

Name Recognition, Names 23 to 33

Complete the meanings of the names and check your answers against the list of names on pages 10 and 11. Note your correct and incorrect answers in the box.

23. Ar-Raafi^	24. Al-Mu^iz	26. As-Samee
27. Al-Baseer	28. Al-Hakam	29. Al-Adl
25. Al-Muthil	30. Al. Al-Lateef	31. Al-Khabeer
32. Al-Haleem	33. Al-Azeem	**Correct** ☐ **Incorrect** ☐

Write the missing number and Arabic name for each meaning

. The Constrictor	. The Exalter	. The Dishonourer
. The Honourer	. The All-Seeing	. The Abaser
. The All Knowing	. The Expander	. The All-Hearing
. The Judge	. The Aware	**Correct** ☐ **Incorrect** ☐

Cover the above exercises and then write the correct names with meaning next to each number in the box below.

24.	31.	25.
27.	28.	33.
23.	26.	29.
30.	32.	**Correct** ☐ **Incorrect** ☐

Puzzle, Names 1 to 33

Now you have learnt the names of Allah from 1 to 33, test your knowledge by completing the names below.

1. **Ar-Ra**_ _ _ _ .
2. **Ar-R**_ _ _ _ _.
3. **Al-M**_ _ _ _ _.
4. **Al-Qu**_ _ _ _ _.
5. **As-Sa**_ _ _ _^
6. **Al-M**_ _ _ _.
7. **Al-Mu**_ _ _ _ _ _.
8. **Al-A**_ _ _ _.
9. **Al-J**_ _ _ _ _.
10. **Al-Mut**_ _ _ _ _ _ _.
11. **Al-K**_ _ _ _ _ _.
12. **Al-B**_ _ _.
13. **Al-Mus**_ _ _ _ _.
14. **Al-G**_ _ _ _ _ _.
15. **Al-Q**_ _ _ _ _.
16. **Al-W**_ _ _ _ _.
17. **Al- R**_ _ _ _ _.
8. **Al- F**_ _ _ _ _.
19. **Al-A**_ _ _ _.
20. **Al-Qa**_ _ _ _.
21. **Al-B**_ _ _ _ _.
22. **Al-Kh**_ _ _ _ _.
23. **Ar-R**_ _ _ _ ^.
24. **Al-Mu^**_ _.
25. **Al-Mut**_ _ _ .
26. **As-S**_ _ _ _ _ ^.
27. **Al-Ba**_ _ _ _.
28. **Al- H** _ _ _ _.
29. **Al-A**_ _.
30. **Al-L**_ _ _ _ _ .
31. **Al-Kh**_ _ _ _ _.
32. **Al-H**_ _ _ _ _.
33. **Al-^Az**_ _ _.

Did you struggle with any? Write down the ones you had difficulty with. Spend 10 minutes re-capping on these.

Number	Name	Meaning

Wordsearch - Names 1 to 33

See how many names you can find in the word search.
(Answers can be found on page 59)

q	w	e	r	t	y	y	u	u	i	o	p	a	s	d	f	g	h	j	k
a	l	m	u	s	a	w	w	i	r	a	l	j	a	b	b	a	r	l	a
s	d	f	g	a	r	r	a	z	z	a	q	h	l	j	k	a	a	o	l
s	z	x	c	v	a	l	b	a	a	s	i	t	m	h	j	s	l	u	a
a	l	m	u	i	z	b	n	m	l	j	q	g	u	a	e	s	a	a	d
l	a	e	a	t	a	l	m	u	m	i	n	r	h	l	a	a	z	l	l
a	l	a	l	e	e	m	e	r	l	t	i	y	a	b	l	m	e	w	u
a	m	l	m	s	d	f	g	a	l	b	a	r	i	a	l	e	e	a	h
m	u	h	a	w	e	r	a	t	b	y	r	u	m	s	a	e	m	h	a
a	t	a	l	x	c	h	v	a	b	a	n	m	i	e	t	a	k	a	r
l	h	l	i	r	k	y	k	u	a	i	l	o	n	e	e	l	p	a	r
f	i	e	k	l	w	a	r	h	t	y	u	k	i	r	e	g	o	b	a
a	l	e	a	o	t	p	a	z	x	c	v	b	h	n	f	h	m	j	h
t	q	m	w	u	e	q	a	l	a	z	e	e	z	a	l	a	k	j	e
t	z	x	m	c	l	v	b	a	l	h	a	k	a	m	a	f	d	f	e
a	c	l	v	a	b	a	l	k	h	a	b	e	e	r	y	f	e	s	m
h	a	l	q	a	a	b	i	d	a	r	r	a	a	f	i	a	i	x	z
a	l	q	u	d	o	o	s	a	r	r	a	h	m	a	n	r	w	d	q

1. Ar-Rahman
2. Ar-Raheem
3. Al-Malik
4. Al-Qudoos
5. As-Salaam
6. Al-Mu'min
7. Al-Muhaimin
8. Al-Azeez
9. Al-Jabbar
10. Al-Mutakabbir
11. Al-Khaaliq
12. Al-Bari
13. Al-Musawwir
14. Al-Ghaffar
15. Al-Qahaar
16. Al-Wahaab
17. Ar-Razzaaq
18. Al-Fattaah
19. Al-Aleem
20. Al-Qaabid
21. Al-Baasit
22. Al-Khafid
23. Ar-Raafi
24. Al-Muiz
25. Al-Muthil
26. As-Samee
27. Al-Baseer
28. Al-Hakam
29. Al-Adl
30. Al-Lateef
31. Al-Khabeer
32. Al-Haleem
33. Al-Azeem

Mind Map - Names 1 to 33

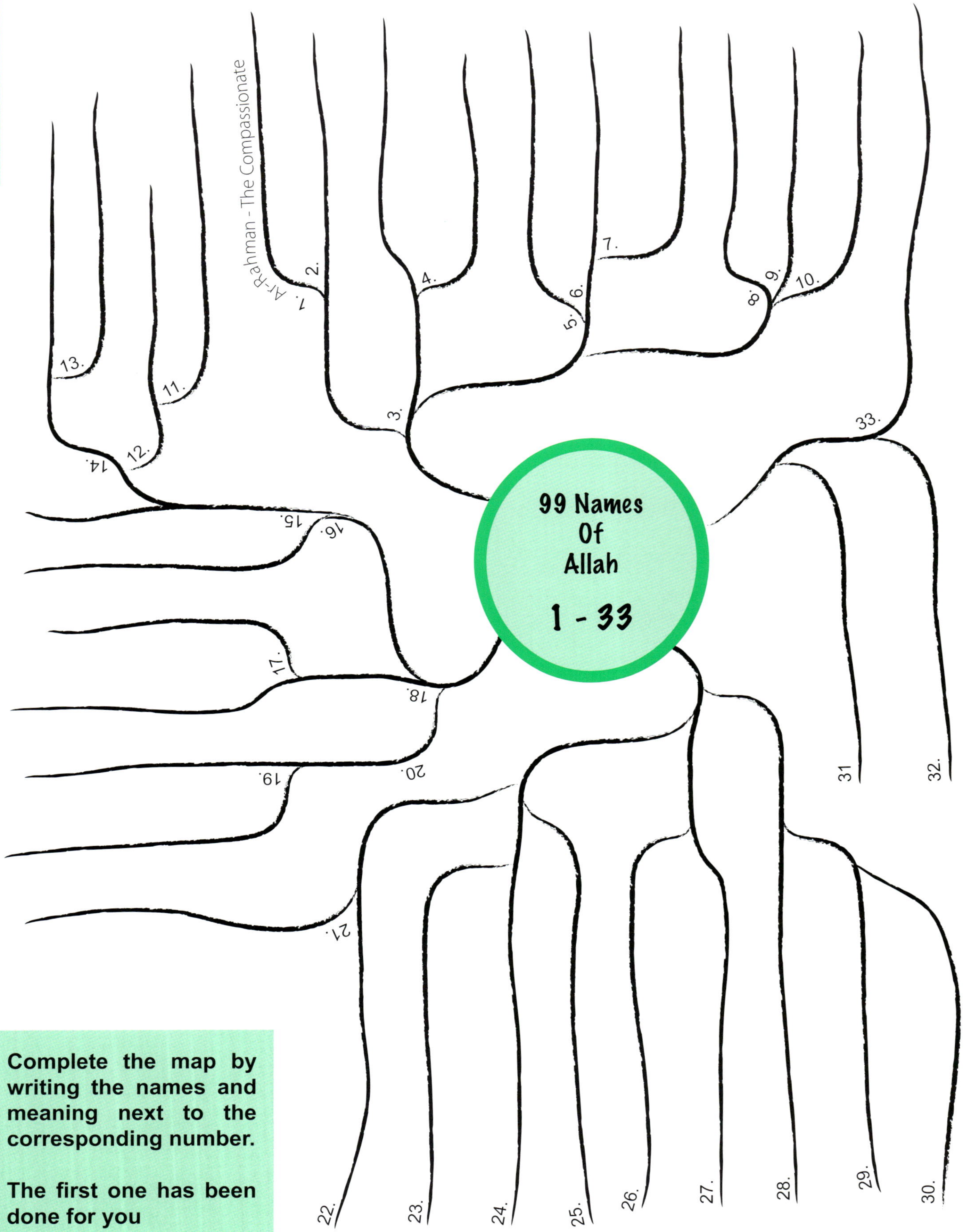

Complete the map by writing the names and meaning next to the corresponding number.

The first one has been done for you

Memorisation List, Names 34 to 44

Start by practising the names of Allah in the following way.

1. Write each number, name and meaning 10 times and in order on a separate piece of paper.
2. Verbally recite each number, name and meaning out loud.
3. When you are confident you have memorised them, update the Progress Chart.

Number	Name	Meaning
34	Al-Ghafoor	The All Forgiving
35	Ash-Shakoor	The Grateful
36	Al-^Aliyy	The Most High
37	Al-Kabeer	The Most Great

Written exercise completed ☐ Oral Memorisation completed ☐ Progress chart completed ☐

Number	Name	Meaning
38	Al-Hafeez	The Preserver
39	Al-Muqeet	The Maintainer
40	Al-Haseeb	The Reckoner
41	Al-Jaleel	The Sublime One

Written exercise completed ☐ Oral Memorisation completed ☐ Progress chart completed ☐

Number	Name	Meaning
42	Al-Kareem	The Generous One
43	Ar-Raqeeb	The Watcher
44	Al-Mujeeb	The Responsive

Written exercise completed ☐ Oral Memorisation completed ☐ Progress chart completed ☐

Learning tip –

"I learn best when I can focus on something visual. So I found the written worksheets extremely helpful. Writing them helped me to recognise the names and meanings, both in order and randomly. By the end of the 5 weeks, the names were ingrained in my memory."
Rebecca, mum to 2

Memorisation List, Names 45 to 55

Start by practising the names of Allah in the following way.

1. Write each number, name and meaning 10 times and in order on a separate piece of paper.
2. Verbally recite each number, name and meaning out loud.
3. When you are confident you have memorised them, update the Progress Chart.

Number	Name	Meaning
45	Al-Wasi	The Vast
46	Al-Hakeem	The Wise
47	Al-Wadood	The Loving
48	Al-Majeed	The Most Glorious

Written exercise completed ☐ Oral Memorisation completed ☐ Progress chart completed ☐

Number	Name	Meaning
49	Al-Ba^ith	The Resurrector
50	Ash-Shaheed	The Witness
51	Al-Haqq	The Truth
52	Al-Wakeel	The Trustee

Written exercise completed ☐ Oral Memorisation completed ☐ Progress chart completed ☐

Number	Name	Meaning
53	Al-Qawiyy	The Most Strong
54	Al-Mateen	The Firm One
55	Al-Waliyy	The Protecting Friend

Written exercise completed ☐ Oral Memorisation completed ☐ Progress chart completed ☐

Learning tip –

"Siblings can verbally test each other on the school run e.g. what is number 17? What does Al- Jaleel mean? What is the Arabic name for The Honourer? I used to do it while driving with my daughters." ***Aneesa, mum to 3***

The 99 Club©

Certificate of Achievement

Awarded to

....

For successfully learning the 99 Names of Allah (SWT)
Asma-Ul-Husna

Congratulations on your achievement!

ASR Ink

Date ....

No:	Name	Meaning

No:	Name	Meaning

No:	Name	Meaning

No:	Name	Meaning

No:	Name	Meaning

No:	Name	Meaning

No:	Name	Meaning

No:	Name	Meaning

Memorisation List, Names 56 to 66

Start by practising the names of Allah in the following way.

1. Write each number, name and meaning 10 times and in order on a separate piece of paper.
2. Verbally recite each number, name and meaning out loud.
3. When you are confident you have memorised them, update the Progress Chart.

Number	Name	Meaning
56	Al-Hameed	The Praiseworthy
57	Al-Muhsee	The Counter
58	Al-Mubdi	The Originator
59	Al-Mu^eed	The Reproducer

Written exercise completed ☐ Oral Memorisation completed ☐ Progress chart completed ☐

Number	Name	Meaning
60	Al-Muhyi	The Restorer
61	Al-Mumeet	The Creator of Death
62	Al-Hayy	The Alive
63	Al-Qayyoom	The Self-Subsisting

Written exercise completed ☐ Oral Memorisation completed ☐ Progress chart completed ☐

Number	Name	Meaning
64	Al-Wajid	The Perceiver
65	Al-Majid	The Illustrious
66	Al-Wahid	The Unique

Written exercise completed ☐ Oral Memorisation completed ☐ Progress chart completed ☐

Learning tip –

"I crammed at the end. I know it's not the best way but I missed a few days as I was ill so I learnt 38 names in the last week. I had to work really hard but it was worth the effort – I didn't want my younger sister to beat me!" ***Shahnaz, 19, university student***

Name Recognition, Names 34 to 44

Complete the meanings of the names and check your answers against the list of names on pages 11 and 12. Note your correct and incorrect answers in the box.

38. Al-Hafeez	41. Aj-Jalil	35. Ash-Shakoor
42. Al-Kareem	34. Al-Ghafoor	40. Al-Haseeb
43. Ar-Raqeeb	39. Al-Muqeet	37. Al-Kabeer
36. Al-^Aliyy	44. Al-Mujeeb	**Correct** ☐ **Incorrect** ☐

Write the missing number and Arabic name for each meaning

. The Watcher	. The All Forgiving	. The Sublime One
. The Preserver	. The Maintainer	. The Most High
. The Grateful	. The Responsive	. The Generous One
. The Reckoner	. The Most Great	**Correct** ☐ **Incorrect** ☐

Cover the above 2 exercises and then write the correct names with meaning next to each number in the box below.

43	36	39
34	44	38
41	37	35
42	40	**Correct** ☐ **Incorrect** ☐

Name Recognition, Names 45 to 55

Complete the meanings of the names and check your answers against the list of names on page 12 and 13. Note your correct and incorrect answers in the box.

50. Ash-Shaheed	47. Al-Wadood	53. Al-Qawiyy
55.Al-Waliyy	51. Al-Haqq	45. Al-Wasi^
46. Al-Hakeem	54. Al-Mateen	48. Al-Majeed
49. Al-Ba^ith	52. Al-Wakeel	**Correct** ☐ **Incorrect** ☐

Write the missing number and Arabic name for each meaning

. The Vast	. The Truth	. The Glorious
. The Trustee	. The Resurrector	. The Firm
. The Loving	. The Strong	. The Wise
. The Witness	. The Protecting Friend	**Correct** ☐ **Incorrect** ☐

Cover the above 2 exercises and then write the correct names with meaning next to each number in the box below.

51	53	46
45	49	50
48	55	54
52	47	**Correct** ☐ **Incorrect** ☐

Name Recognition, Names 56 to 66

Complete the meanings of the names and check your answers against the list of names on pages 13. Note your correct and incorrect answers in the box.

59. Al-Mu^eed	61. Al-Mumeet	58. Al-Mubdi
62. Al-Hayy	56. Al-Hameed	63. Al-Qayyoom
57. Al-Muhsee	64. Al-Wajid	60. Al-Muhyi
66. Al-Wahid	65. Al-Majid	**Correct** ☐ **Incorrect** ☐

Write the missing number and Arabic name for each meaning

. The Reproducer	. The Creator of Death	. The Illustrious
. The Praiseworthy	. The Unique	. The Restorer
. The Alive	. The Originator	. The Perceiver
. The Counter	. The Self-Subsisting	**Correct** ☐ **Incorrect** ☐

Cover the above 2 exercises and then write the correct names with meaning next to each number in the box below.

65	58	66
57	63	64
59	61	56
62	60	**Correct** ☐ **Incorrect** ☐

Puzzle, Names 34 to 66

Now you have learnt the names of Allah from 34 to 66, test your knowledge by completing the names below.

34. **Al- G_ _ _ _ _ _ _.**
35. **Ash-S_ _ _ _ _ _.**
36. **Al-A_ _ _ _.**
37. **Al-K_ _ _ _ _.**
38. **Al-Ha_ _ _ _.**
39. **Al-M_ _ _ _ _.**
40. **Al-Has_ _ _.**
41. **Aj-J_ _ _ _ _.**
42. **Al-Ka_ _ _ _.**
43. **Ar-R_ _ _ _ _.**
44. **Al-Mu_ _ _ _.**
45. **Al-W_ _ _ ^.**
46. **Al- Hak_ _ _.**
47. **Al-Wa_ _ _ _.**
48. **Al-Ma_ _ _ _.**
49. **Al-B_ _ ^ _ _.**
50. **Ash-S_ _ _ _ _ _ _.**
51. **Al-H_ _ _.**
52. **Al-W_ _ _ _ _.**
53. **Al-Q_ _ _ _ _.**
54. **Al-Ma_ _ _ _.**
55. **Al-W_ _ _ _ _.**
56. **Al-H_ _ _ _ _.**
57. **Al-M_ _ _ _ _.**
58. **Al-Mu_ _ _.**
59. **Al-M_ ^_ _ _.**
60. **Al-Muh_ _ .**
61. **Al-Mum_ _ _.**
62. **Al-H_ _ _.**
63. **Al-Qa_ _ _ _ _.**
64. **Al- Wa _ _ _ _.**
65. **Al-M _ _ _ _ _.**
66. **Al- Wa_ _ _ _.**

Did you struggle with any? Write down the ones you had difficulty with. Spend 10 minutes re-capping on these.

Number	Name	Meaning

Wordsearch - Names 34 to 66

See how many names you can find in the word search.
(Answers can be found on page 59)

a	l	m	u	b	a	i	t	x	a	l	m	a	j	e	e	d	r	g	a
l	x	c	r	a	l	w	a	h	i	d	v	y	a	d	a	a	a	u	l
m	a	a	a	l	q	a	g	s	w	u	m	i	l	f	j	l	l	y	h
u	l	l	l	w	a	s	a	n	h	p	o	j	w	l	j	m	w	e	a
b	q	w	m	a	y	h	l	l	u	s	n	x	a	b	a	u	a	u	f
d	a	a	u	d	y	s	h	i	g	z	h	d	s	l	l	h	k	a	e
i	w	j	q	o	o	h	a	u	a	h	g	a	i	s	e	s	e	l	e
a	i	i	e	o	o	a	k	a	l	r	a	u	h	c	e	e	e	b	z
l	y	d	e	d	m	k	e	l	m	a	r	f	v	e	l	e	l	a	a
m	y	h	t	y	o	o	e	m	u	m	l	a	f	y	e	q	a	i	l
u	w	z	b	r	d	o	m	u	e	c	s	h	q	o	y	d	l	t	h
m	q	s	d	g	c	r	v	j	e	g	h	j	a	e	o	l	m	h	a
e	a	l	a	l	i	y	y	e	d	y	u	i	o	q	e	r	a	z	y
e	s	d	a	l	k	a	r	e	e	m	g	n	c	w	q	b	j	r	y
t	a	l	h	a	s	e	e	b	a	l	m	a	t	e	e	n	i	b	l
a	l	k	a	b	e	e	r	y	a	l	w	a	l	i	y	y	d	h	g
a	l	m	u	h	y	i	a	l	h	a	m	e	e	d	y	s	b	e	k
p	h	r	e	w	q	p	l	k	j	m	n	c	w	y	p	t	v	g	d

34. Al-Ghaffoor
35. Ash-Shakoor
36. Al-Aliyy
37. Al-Kabeer
38. Al-Hafeez
39. Al-Muqeet
40. Al-Haseeb
41. Aj-Jaleel
42. Al-Kareem
43. Ar-Raqeeb
44. Al-Mujeeb
45. Al-Wasi
46. Al-Hakeem
47. Al-Wadood
48. Al-Majeed
49. Al-Baith
50. Ash-Shaheed
51. Al-Haqq
52. Al-Wakeel
53. Al-Qawiyy
54. Al-Mateen
55. Al-Waliyy
56. Al-Hameed
57. Al-Muhsee
58. Al-Mubdi
59. Al-Mueed
60. Al-Muhyi
61. Al-Mumeet
62. Al-Hayy
63. Al-Qayyoom
64. Al-Wajid
65. Al-Majid
66. Al-Wahid

Mind Map Names - 1 to 66

Complete the map by writing the names and meaning next to the corresponding number. The first one has been done for you

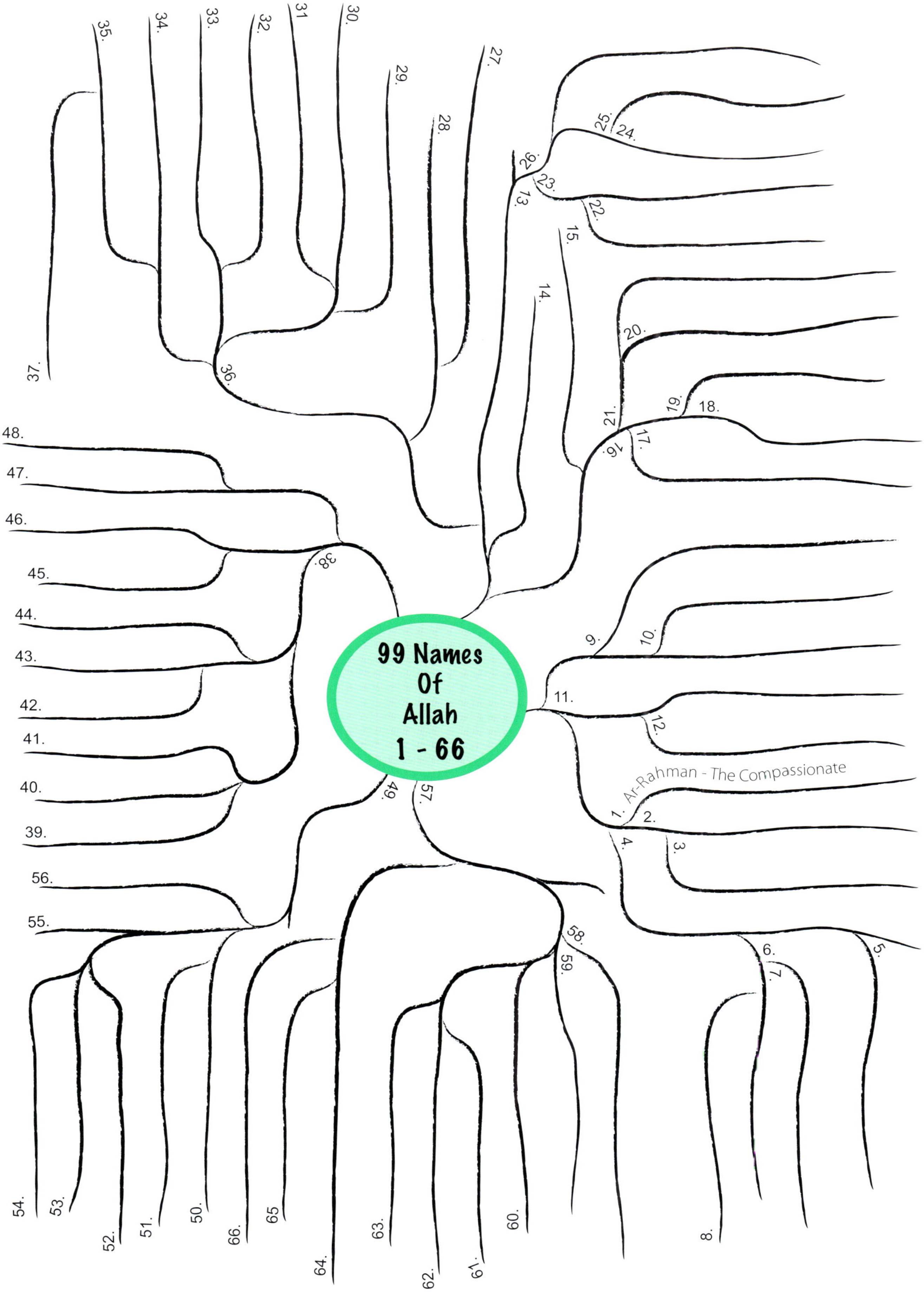

Memorisation List, Names 67 to 77

Start by practising the names of Allah in the following way.

1. Write each number, name and meaning 10 times and in order on a separate piece of paper.
2. Verbally recite each number, name and meaning out loud.
3. When you are confident you have memorised them, update the Progress Chart.

Number	Name	Meaning
67	Al-Ahad	The One
68	As-Samad	The Eternal
69	Al-Qaadir	The Able
70	Al-Muqtadir	The Powerful

Written exercise completed ☐ Oral Memorisation completed ☐ Progress chart completed ☐

Number	Name	Meaning
71	Al-Muqaddim	The Expediter
72	Al-Mu'akh-hir	The Delayer
73	Al-Awwal	The First
74	Al-Akhir	The Last

Written exercise completed ☐ Oral Memorisation completed ☐ Progress chart completed ☐

Number	Name	Meaning
75	Az-Zaahir	The Manifest
76	Al-Baatin	The Hidden
77	Al-Walee	The Governor

Written exercise completed ☐ Oral Memorisation completed ☐ Progress chart completed ☐

Learning tip –

"I found the mind maps the best. After completing each one, I could see what I needed to revise more such as concentrate on the 40's section or the names beginning with M or had forgotten and what I had learnt well. Only when I was confident I knew the names did I move on to the next section. It really focussed me." Sabreen, 15

Memorisation List, Names 78 to 88

Start by practising the names of Allah in the following way.

1. Write each number, name and meaning 10 times and in order on a separate piece of paper.
2. Verbally recite each number, name and meaning out loud.
3. When you are confident you have memorised them, update the Progress Chart.

Number	Name	Meaning
78	Al-Muta^ali	The Most Exalted
79	Al-Baar	The Source of All Goodness
80	At-Tawwaab	The Acceptor of Repentance
81	Al-Muntaqim	The Avenger

Written exercise completed ☐ Oral Memorisation completed ☐ Progress chart completed ☐

Number	Name	Meaning
82	Al-^Afuww	The Pardoner
83	Ar-Ra'uf	The Compassionate
84	Malik Al-Mulk	The Eternal Owner of Sovereignty
85	Thul-Jalali wal Ikram	The Lord of Majesty and Bounty

Written exercise completed ☐ Oral Memorisation completed ☐ Progress chart completed ☐

Number	Name	Meaning
86	Al- Muqsit	The Equitable
87	Aj-Jaami^	The Gatherer
88	Al-Ghaniyy	The Self-Sufficient

Written exercise completed ☐ Oral Memorisation completed ☐ Progress chart completed ☐

Learning tip –

"Doing this challenge made me realise how I learn best: straight after breakfast! As it was the holidays, I didn't have to go to school (yay!) so after brekkie, I'd sit at the table, do my workbook, learn the 3 names for the day, quickly look over the ones I'd already learnt and that was it! I was free for the rest of the day on my Nintendo…" ***Hassan, 8***

Memorisation List, Names 89 to 99

Start by practising the names of Allah in the following way.

1. Write each number, name and meaning 10 times and in order on a separate piece of paper.
2. Verbally recite each number, name and meaning out loud.
3. When you are confident you have memorised them, update the Progress Chart.

Number	Name	Meaning
89	Al-Mughni	The Enricher
90	Al-Maani^	The Preventer
91	Ad-Daarr	The Distresser
92	An-Nafi^	The Benefactor

Written exercise completed ☐ Oral Memorisation completed ☐ Progress chart completed ☐

Number	Name	Meaning
93	An-Noor	The Light
94	Al-Haadi	The Guide
95	Al-Badi^	The Incomparable
96	Al-Baaqi	The Evelasting

Written exercise completed ☐ Oral Memorisation completed ☐ Progress chart completed ☐

Number	Name	Meaning
97	Al-Waarith	The Supreme Inheritor
98	Ar-Rasheed	The Guide to the Right Path
99	As-Saboor	The Patient

Written exercise completed ☐ Oral Memorisation completed ☐ Progress chart completed ☐

Learning tip –

"Learn at your own pace and don't pressurise yourself. It's not a competition." ***Maeesha, 11.***

Name Recognition, Names 67 to 77

Complete the meanings of the names and check your answers against the list of names on pages 14. Note your correct and incorrect answers in the box.

67. Al-Ahad	69. The Qaadir	71. Al-Muqaddim
70. Al-Muqtadir	72. Al-Mu'akh-khir	74. Al-Akhir.
68. As-Samad	76. Al-Baatin	73. Al-Awwal
75. Az-Zaahir	77. Al-Walee	**Correct** ☐ **Incorrect** ☐

Write the missing number and Arabic name for each meaning

. The Governor	. The Eternal	. The First
. The Manifest	. The Delayer	. The Hidden
. The One	. The Expediter	. The Able
. The Last	. The Powerful	**Correct** ☐ **Incorrect** ☐

Cover the above 2 exercises and then write the correct names with meaning next to each number in the box below.

70.	68.	76.
75.	71.	73.
72.	67.	69.
77.	74.	**Correct** ☐ **Incorrect** ☐

Name Recognition, Names 78 - 88

Complete the meanings of the names and check your answers against the list of names on page 14 and 15. Note your correct and incorrect answers in the box.

84.Malik-al-Mulk	81.Al-Muntaqim	78. Al-Muta'ali.
88. Al-Ghaniyy	87. Aj-Jaami	82. Al-Afuww
80. At-Tawwaab	79. Al-Barr	83. Ar-Ra'uf
85. Thul-Jalali- wal-Ikram	86. Al-Muqsit	**Correct** ☐ **Incorrect** ☐

Write the missing number and Arabic name for each meaning

. The Most Exhalted	. The Acceptor of Repentance	. The Equitable
. The Owner of Sovereignty	. The Compassionate	. The Pardoner
. The Avenger	. The Gatherer	. The Source of All Goodness
. The Self-Sufficient	. The Lord of Majesty & Bounty	**Correct** ☐ **Incorrect** ☐

Cover the above 2 exercises and then write the correct names with meaning next to each number in the box below.

80.	87.	83.
86.	81.	88.
82.	79.	84.
78.	85.	**Correct** ☐ **Incorrect** ☐

Name Recognition, Names 89 - 99

Complete the meanings of the names and check your answers against the list of names on pages 15 and 16. Note your correct and incorrect answers in the box.

92. An-Nafi^	95. Al-Badi^	90. Al-Maani
96. Al-Baaqi	93. An-Noor	94.Al-Haadi
89. Al-Mughni	98. Ar-Rasheed	91. Ad-Daarr
97. Al-Waarith.	99. As-Saboor.	**Correct** ☐ **Incorrect** ☐

Write the missing number and Arabic name for each meaning

. The Distresser	. The Light	. The Supreme Inheritor
. The Guide	. The Preventer	. Ar-Rasheed
. The Patient	. The Incomparable	. The Benefactor
. The Enricher	. The Everlasting	**Correct** ☐ **Incorrect** ☐

Cover the above 2 exercises and then write the correct names with meaning next to each number in the box below.

90.	99.	96.
97.	91.	89.
93.	94.	95.
98.	92.	**Correct** ☐ **Incorrect** ☐

Puzzle, Names 67 to 99

Now you have learnt the names of Allah from 1 to 33, test your knowledge by completing the names below.

67. **Al-A** _ _ _.
68. **As-S** _ _ _ _.
69. **Al- Q** _ _ _ _ _.
70. **Al- Mu** _ _ _ _ _ _.
71. **Al-** M _ _ _ _ _ _ _.
72. **Al- Mu'a** _ _ **-** _ _ _ _.
73. **Al- A** _ _ _ _.
74. **Al- Ak** _ _ _ .
75. **Az-Z** _ _ _ _ _.
76. **Al-Ba** _ _ _ _.
77. **Al-W** _ _ _ _.
78. **Al-Mu** _ _ **^** _ _ _.
79. **Al- B** _ _ _.
80. **At- Ta** _ _ _ _ _.
81. **Al-Mun** _ _ _ _ _.
82. **Al-^ Af** _ _ _.
83. **Ar- R** _ **'** _ _.
84. **Malik Al-** _ _ _ _.
85. **Thul-Jalali** _ _ _ **-** _ _ _ _ _ _.
86. **Al-M** _ _ _ _ _.
87. **Aj-J** _ _ _ _.
88. **Al-Gh** _ _ _ _ _ .
89. **Al- Mug** _ _ _.
90. **Al- Ma** _ _ _.
91. **Ad - D** _ _ _ _.
92. **An-N** _ _ _ **^**.
93. **Al-N** _ _ _ _.
94. **Al- H** _ _ _ _.
95. Al- **Ba** _ _ **^**.
96. **Al- B** _ _ _ _.
97. **Al-Wa** _ _ _ _ _.
98. **Ar-R** _ _ _ _ _ _ _.
99. **As-Sa** _ _ _ _

Did you struggle with any? Write down the ones you had difficulty with. Spend 10 minutes re-capping on these.

Number	Name	Meaning

Wordsearch - Names 67 to 99

See how many names you can find in the word search.
(Answers can be found on page 59)

l	h	a	a	r	a	c	a	r	r	a	s	h	e	e	d	k	d	p	a
a	a	a	l	l	p	t	w	r	a	l	h	a	a	d	i	y	h	q	l
l	t	l	l	g	m	v	t	o	t	a	d	d	a	a	r	r	a	j	m
m	a	a	m	m	h	a	p	a	q	f	h	d	w	m	e	h	r	l	u
u	s	l	s	u	u	a	a	e	w	u	k	r	e	j	a	f	r	o	t
g	s	w	m	s	k	q	n	n	r	w	s	y	k	d	l	c	a	b	a
h	a	a	a	u	a	t	a	i	i	w	a	i	a	n	a	l	u	d	a
n	m	a	n	l	n	b	a	d	y	t	o	a	l	n	h	g	f	s	l
i	a	r	n		b	t	o	d	d	y	a	l	b	a	a	t	i	n	i
g	d	i	o	r	e	a	a	o	i	i	x	u	a	c	d	t	a	a	a
t	z	t	o	f	v	p	a	q	r	r	m	b	r	a	x	e	n	l	l
o	l	h	r	m	d	e	w	q	i	k	a	j	r	l	e	s	n	a	a
a	z	z	a	a	h	i	r	d	i	m	p	f	v	t	o	d	a	k	w
h	u	q	s	n	o	a	l	m	u	a	k	h	k	h	i	r	f	h	w
a	l	w	a	l	e	e	a	j	j	a	a	m	i	s	t	r	i	i	a
a	l	q	a	a	d	i	r	a	l	b	a	d	i	x	l	y	z	r	l
a	l	m	u	q	s	i	t	e	m	a	l	i	k	a	l	m	u	l	k
t	h	u	l	j	a	l	a	l	i	w	a	l	i	k	r	a	m	g	h

67. Al-Ahad
68. As-Samad
69. Al-Qaadir
70. Al-Muqtadir
71. Al-Muqaddim
72. Al-Mu'akh-khir
73. Al-Awwal
74. Al-Akhir
75. Az-Zaahir
76. Al-Baatin
77. Al-Walee
78. Al-Muta-ali
79. Al-Barr
80. At-Tawwaab
81. Al -Muntaqim
82. Al-Afuww
83. Ar-Ra'uf
84. Malik Al-Mulk
85. Thul Jalali wal-Ikram
86. Al-Muqsit
87. Aj-Jaami
88. Al-Ghaniyy
89. Al-Mughni
90. Al-Maani
91. Ad-Daarr
92. An-Nafi
93. An-Noor
94. Al-Haadi
95. Al-Badi
96. Al-Baaqi
97. Al-Waarith
98. Ar-Rasheed
99. As-Saboor

Worksheet 27

Mind Map - Names 1 to 99

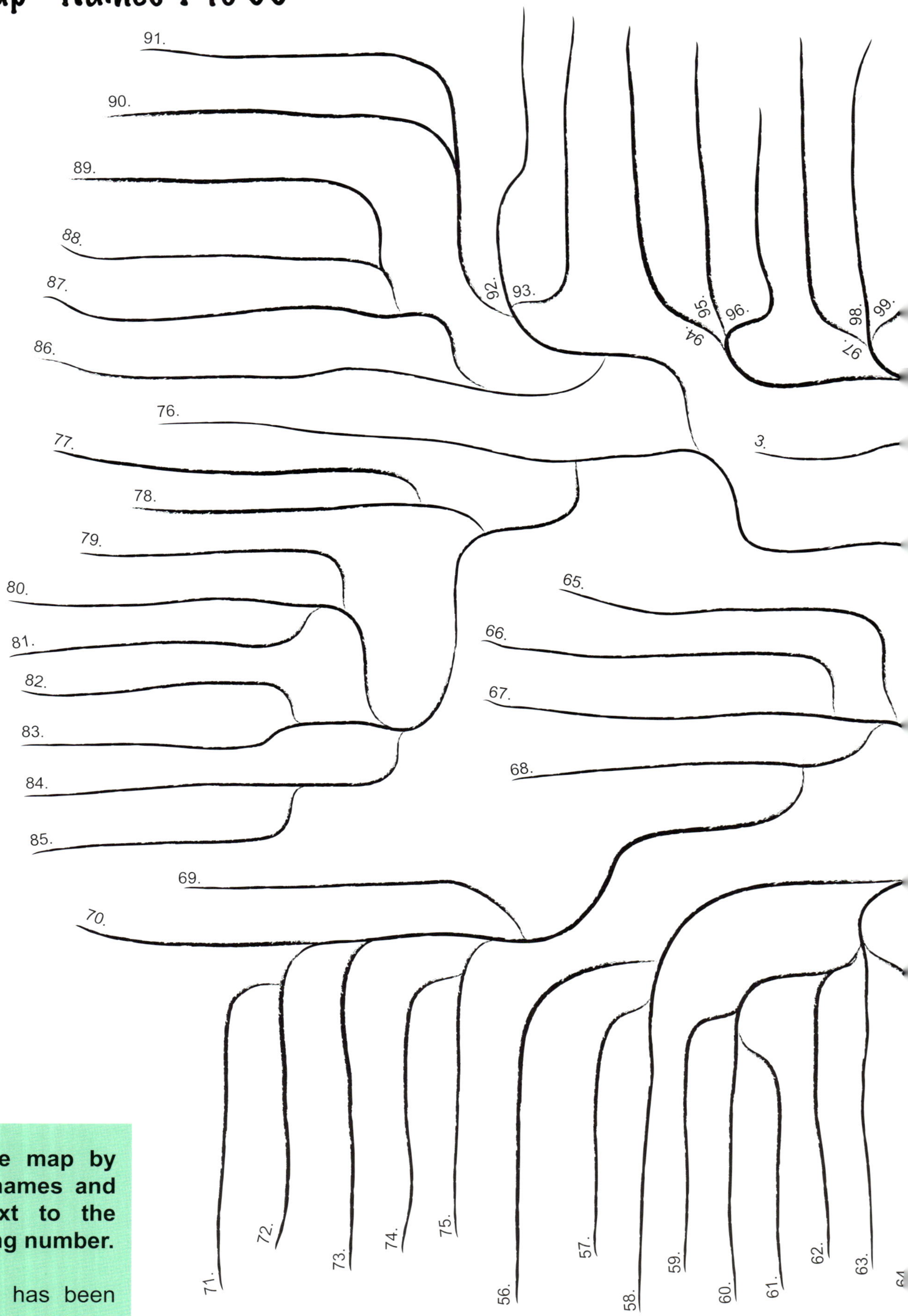

Complete the map by writing the names and meaning next to the corresponding number.

The first one has been done for you

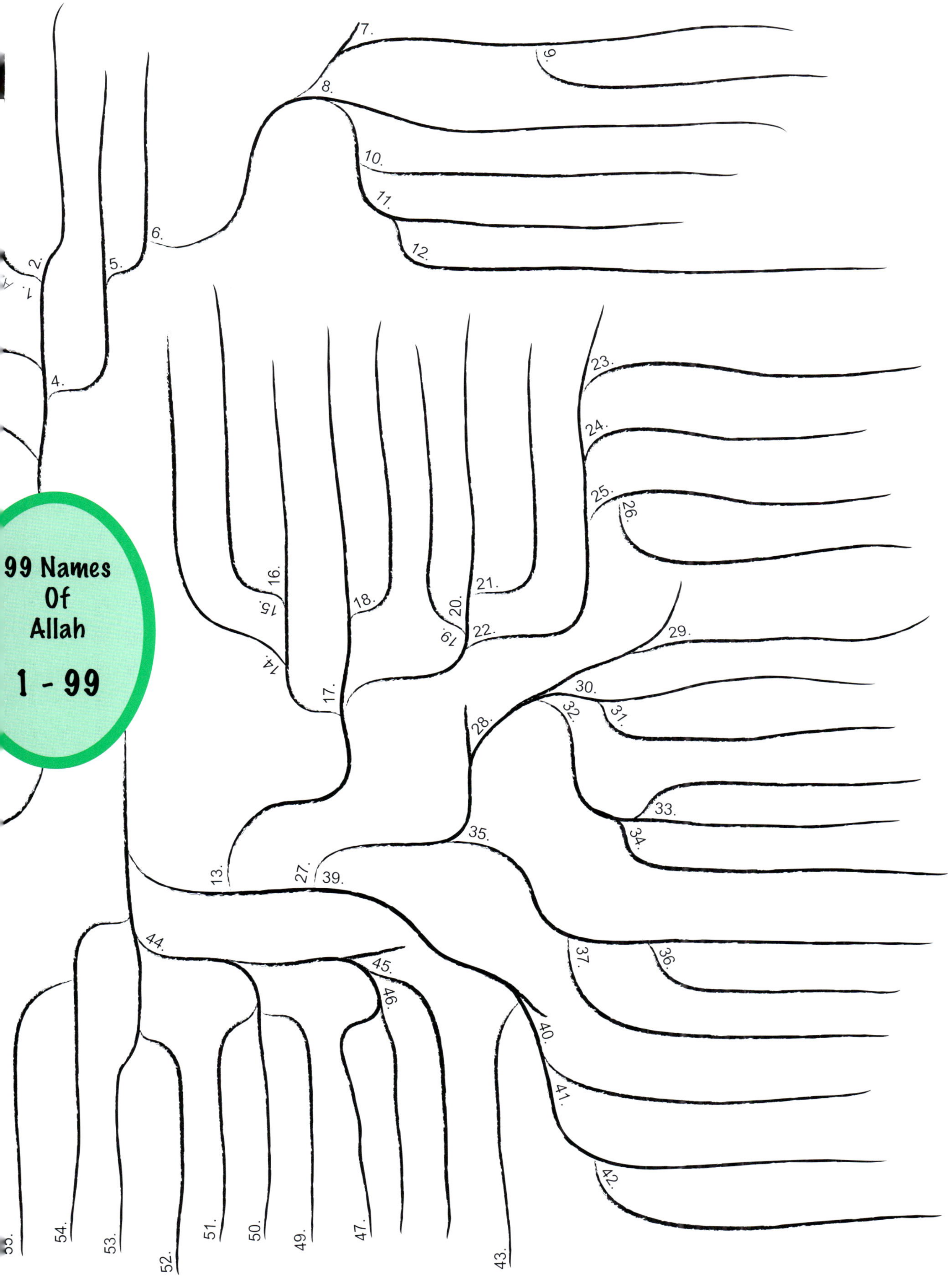
99 Names
Of
Allah
1 - 99

Memorisation Record

Can you recite all the names you know from 1 – 25 in 1 minute.

Use the card to help you learn. Repeat this exercise until you notice your time improving. Keep a record of your times and set yourself a target time for the next time your practise. Do this approximately twice per week.

Date	Best Time	Target For Next Time

Final Written Test, Names 1 to 99

You are now ready for your final test.

1. Begin with Bismillahir Rahman ir Raheem.
2. There is no time limit to complete the test.
3. The object of the test is to see how many names you have learnt. Insha'Allah, you will have learnt all of them
4. If you find you've missed some, don't worry.
5. You can go back, practise some more and re-sit the test. There are clues to the answers for you.
6. For those of you who are older or if you want to set yourself a harder test, you could simply see how many names you have learnt by writing out in order, numbers, names and meanings from 1 to 99 on a separate piece of paper.
7. Mark your answers against the list of names and meanings beginning on page 9.

Children's tests should be marked by an adult or the group leader.

Number	Name	Meaning
1	**Ar- R**	The C
2	**Ar-R**	The M
3	**Al-M**	The K
4	**Al-Q**	The H
5	**As-S**	The S
6	**Al-M**	The G
7	**Al-M**	The P
8	**Al-^A**	The M
9	**Al-J**	The C
10	**Al-M**	The M
11	**Al-K**	The C
12	**Al-B**	The E

13	**Al-M**	The F
14	**Al-G**	The G
15	**Al-Q**	The S
16	**Al-W**	The B
17	**Ar-R**	The S
18	**Al-F**	The O
19	**Al-^A**	The A
20	**Al-Q**	The C
21	**Al-B**	The E
22	**Al-K**	The A
23	**Ar-R**	The E
24	**Al-M**	The H
25	**Al-M**	The D
26	**As-S**	The A
27	**Al-B**	The A
28	**Al-H**	The J
29	**Al-^A**	The J
30	**Al-L**	The S
31	**Al-K**	The A
32	**Al-H**	The F
33	**Al-^A**	The G
34	**Al-G**	The A

35	**Ash-S**	The G
36	**Al-^A**	The M
37	**Al-K**	The M
38	**Al-H**	The P
39	**Al-M**	The M
40	**Al-H**	The R
41	**Aj-J**	The S
42	**Al-K**	The G
43	**Ar-R**	The W
44	**Al-M**	The R
45	**Al-W**	The V
46	**Al-H**	The W
47	**Al-W**	The L
48	**Al-M**	The M
49	**Al-B**	The R
50	**Ash-S**	The W
51	**Al-H**	The T
52	**Al-W**	The T
53	**Al-Q**	The M
54	**Al-M**	The F
55	**Al-W**	The P
56	**Al-H**	The P

57	**Al-M**	The C
58	**Al-M**	The O
59	**Al-M**	The R
60	**Al-M**	The R
61	**Al-M**	The C
62	**Al-H**	The A
63	**Al-Q**	The S
64	**Al-W**	The P
65	**Al-M**	The I
66	**Al-W**	The U
67	**Al-A**	The O
68	**As-S**	The E
69	**Al-Q**	The A
70	**Al-M**	The P
71	**Al-M**	The E
72	**Al-M**	The D
73	**Al-'A**	The F
74	**Al-'A**	The L
75	**Az-Z**	The M
76	**Al-B**	The H
77	**Al-W**	The G
78	**Al-M**	The M

79	**Al-B**	The S
80	**At-T**	The A
81	**Al-M**	The A
82	**Al-^A**	The P
83	**Ar-R**	The C
84	**M**	The E
85	**T**	The L
86	**Al-M**	The E
87	**Aj-J**	The G
88	**Al-G**	The S
89	**Al-M**	The E
90	**Al-M**	The P
91	**Ad-D**	The D
92	**An-N**	The B
93	**An-N**	The L
94	**Al-H**	The G
95	**Al-B**	The I
96	**Al-B**	The E
97	**Al-W**	The S
98	**Ar-R**	The G
99	**As-S**	The P

Now check your answers against the 99 Names list on pages 9-16 .

Correct answers	☐	Incorrect answers	☐

List the incorrect answers and revise these again:

Oral Test

It is also helpful if you can have an oral recitation test. Ask someone to listen to you recite and compare against the list of 99 Names on pages 9 -16.

Correct answers	☐	Incorrect answers	☐

Revise any incorrect answers and use the table below to monitor your revision.

Date	Names To Revise	Revision completed	Date tested: Number correct: Number Incorrect:

Log of Future Practice

Now that you have insha'Allah memorised the 99 names, it is important that you maintain your knowledge. Use this record sheet to keep practising the names until you are satisfied that the names are permanently ingrained in your memory.

Date	Names Practiced	Names To Work On

Notes:

Notes:

Wordsearch - SOLUTIONS

Anwers to the wordsearch featured on page 27

q	w	e	r	t	y	y	u	u	i	o	p	a	s	d	f	g	h	j	k
a	l	m	u	s	a	w	w	i	r	a	l	j	a	b	b	a	r	l	a
s	d	f	g	a	r	r	a	z	z	a	q	h	l	j	k	a	a	o	l
s	z	x	c	v	a	l	b	a	a	s	i	t	m	h	j	s	l	u	a
a	l	m	u	i	z	b	n	m	l	j	q	g	u	a	e	s	a	a	d
l	a	e	a	t	a	l	m	u	m	i	n	r	h	l	a	a	z	l	l
a	l	a	l	e	e	m	e	r	l	t	i	y	a	b	l	m	e	w	u
a	m	l	m	s	d	f	g	a	l	b	a	r	i	a	l	e	e	a	h
m	u	h	a	w	e	r	a	t	b	y	r	u	m	s	a	e	m	h	a
a	t	a	l	x	c	h	v	a	b	a	n	m	i	e	t	a	k	a	r
l	h	l	i	r	k	y	k	u	a	i	l	o	n	e	e	l	p	a	r
f	i	e	k	l	w	a	r	h	t	y	u	k	i	r	e	g	o	b	a
a	l	e	a	o	t	p	a	z	x	c	v	b	h	n	f	h	m	j	h
t	q	m	w	u	e	q	a	l	a	z	e	e	z	a	l	a	k	j	e
t	z	x	m	c	l	v	b	a	l	h	a	k	a	m	a	f	d	f	e
a	c	l	v	a	b	a	l	k	h	a	b	e	e	r	y	f	e	s	m
h	a	l	q	a	a	b	i	d	a	r	r	a	a	f	i	a	i	x	z
a	l	q	u	d	o	o	s	a	r	r	a	h	m	a	n	r	w	d	q

Anwers to the wordsearch featured on page 36

a	l	m	u	b	a	i	t	x	a	l	m	a	j	e	e	d	r	g	a
l	x	c	r	a	l	w	a	h		d	v	y	a	d	a	a	a	u	l
m	a	a	a	l	q	a	g	s	w	u	m	i	l	f	j	l	l	y	h
u	l	l	l	w	a	s	a	n	h	p	o	j	w	l	j	m	w	e	a
b	q	w	m	a	y	h	l	l	u	s	n	x	a	b	a	u	a	u	f
d	a	a	u	d	y	s	h	i	g	z	h	d	s	l	l	h	k	a	e
i	w	j	q	o	o	h	a	u	a	h	g	a	i	s	e	s	e	l	e
a	i	i	e	o	o	a	k	a		r	a	u	h	c	e	e	e	b	z
l	y	d	e	d	m	k	e	l	n	a	r	f	v	e	l	e	l	a	a
m	y	h	t	y	o	o	e	m	u	m	l	a	f	y	e	q	a	i	l
u	w	z	b	r	d	o	m	u	e	c	s	h	q	o	y	d	l	t	h
m	q	s	d	g	c	r	v	j	e	g	h	j	a	e	o	l	m	h	a
e	a	l	a	l	i	y	y	e	d	y	u	i	o	q	e	r	a	z	y
e	s	d	a	l	k	a	r	e	e	m	g	n	c	w	q	b	j	r	y
t	a	l	h	a	s	e	e	b	a	l	m	a	t	e	e	n	i	b	l
a	l	k	a	b	e	e	r	y	a	l	w	a	l	i	y	y	d	h	g
a	l	m	u	h	y	i	a	l	h	a	m	e	e	d	y	s	b	e	k
p	h	r	e	w	q	p	l	k	j	m	n	c	w	y	p	t	v	g	d

Anwers to the wordsearch featured on page 45

l	h	a	a	r	a	c	a	r	r	a	s	h	e	e	d	k	d	p	a
a	a	a	l	l	p	t	w	r	a	l	h	a	a	d	i	y	h	q	l
l	t	l	l	g	m	v	t	o		a	d	d	a	a	r	r	a	j	m
m	a	a	m	m	h	a	p	a	q	f	h	d	w	m	e	h	r	l	u
u	s	l	s	u	u	a	a	e	w	u	k	r	e	j	a	f	r	o	t
g	s	w	m	s	k	q	n	n	r	w	s	y	k	d	l	c	a	b	a
h	a	a	a	u	a	t	a	i		w	a	i	a	n	a	l	u	d	a
n	m	a	n	l	n	b	a	d	y	t	o	a	l	n	h	g	f	s	l
i	a	r	n		b	t	o	d	d	y	a	l	b	a	a	t	i	n	i
g	d	i	o	r	e	a	a	o	i	i	x	u	a	c	d	t	a	a	a
t	z	t	o	f	v	p	a	q	r	r	m	b	r	a	x	e	n	l	l
o	l	h	r	m	d	e	w	q	i	k	a	j	r	l	e	s	n	a	a
a	z	z	a	a	h	i	r	d	i	m	p	f	v	t	o	d	a	k	w
h	u	q	s	n	o	a	l	m	u	a	k	h	k	h	i	r	f	h	w
a	l	w	a	l	e	e	a	j	j	a	a	m	i	s	t	r	i	i	a
a	l	q	a	a	d	i	r	a	l	b	a	d	i	x	l	y	z	r	l
a	l	m	u	q	s	i	t	e	m	a	l	i	k	a	l	m	u	l	k
t	h	u	l	j	a	l	a	l	i	w	a	l	i	k	r	a	m	g	h

A 99 Club© Award Ceremony

Now that you have successfully learnt the 99 names of Allah, why don't you consider having a 99 Club© Award Ceremony? By inviting friends and family members, it is a fun and uplifting way of celebrating your success, sharing your achievement with others and encouraging others to also take on the challenge and learn the 99 Names. In addition, it gives you and your child/group a sense of achievement and will, insha'Allah, motivate you all to maintain the knowledge you have acquired by making a positive habit of reciting the names on a daily basis. Remember our Prophet taught that those who learn the 99 names of Allah shall enter Paradise. It is important that you maintain your knowledge.

The 99 Club© offers a celebration pack that will make your celebratory event a delight and add to the theme of the occasion. The Workbook includes a certificate from The 99 Club© that can be presented on the occasion. Public recognition of a child's achievement is fantastic for their self-esteem. We recognize GCSEs and other exam results, why not results for Allah? And if you're an adult but a child at heart, what's stopping you from having one? We know we enjoyed ourselves just as much as our children did. We went on a horse riding party...

The 99 Club and What Happens Next?

The 99 Club© is building an international picture of how many people have used The 99 Club© resources and successfully learnt the 99 Names. It would be amazing to see how many people have learnt the 99 Names of Allah across the world, and why not share tips and ideas on how you achieved this, what problems and struggles you faced, what worked for you and what didn't work so well? We'll also be holding regional and national competitions throughout the year and have fundraisers to put our knowledge to good use, Insha'Allah. Our aim is to constantly develop and improve our resources so we welcome your feedback, comments and suggestions.

Jazak-Allah Khair for taking part in the 99 Name Challenge and congratulations on your fantastic success! Now it's time to share your success with our 99 Club© community and tell us your experience. Log on to www.the99club.net and share your journey with everyone.

You and the Future

Now that you have memorised the 99 Names of Allah – it is not over! It is important that your knowledge is maintained and put to good use. Remember to practise regularly even if it is only once a month. This will in the long term, embed in your memory and hopefully stay with you for life. It is best to try and recite the names at least once each day and at each prayer time. This is a way of glorifying Allah and gaining His pleasure. The 99 Club© is dedicated to helping as many people around the world as possible to learn the 99 names of Allah and we hope you will join us in promoting and encouraging others in follow in your footsteps. If you found this workbook useful, tell others about it so they can reap the same reward. You will insha'Allah gain further rewards from Allah for such a good deed.